IMAGES OF CHARTISM

IMAGES OF CHARTISM

By Stephen Roberts
and
Dorothy Thompson

Merlin Press
1998

First published in 1998
in the UK by The Merlin Press Ltd.
2 Rendlesham Mews
Rendlesham   Woodbridge
Suffolk IP12 2SZ

ISBN 085036 475 2

Designed and set by Julie Rainford

Printed in UK by Biddles Ltd., Guildford, Surrey

CONTENTS

For Philip Walmsley, schoolteacher.

FOREWORD

One hundred and fifty years ago Europe was convulsed by revolution. Nationalist movements overthrew old imperialist thrones and governments. Lawyers, journalists, intellectuals and artisans combined to demand new democratic structures to replace the *anciens regimes* which had regained power in the years since the defeat of Napoleon. Yet in England, the country whose reformed parliamentary system inspired many of the revolutionary impulses of the year of revolutions, no rising took place. The Chartist movement, the greatest combination of working people in Europe, in spite of massive nationwide demonstrations in support of its demands, never seriously threatened established authority in that year.

Much of the historiography of Chartism has presented it as a failed revolutionary movement whose final defeat occurred in 1848. There had certainly been a moment nine years earlier when the government had faced the threat of armed rising and when armed men had marched on a centre of authority to face, and to be defeated by, military action. The most recent account of the 1839 rising in Wales [1] paints the intensity and bitterness of the class conflict that inspired it, and there can be little doubt that the same feelings were to be found in many parts of Britain throughout the 1830s and 1840s. In other parts of the British Empire, particularly in Canada and Ireland, these decades saw the growth of movements in many ways more like those in continental Europe, with similar nationalist and anti-imperialist aims. Nevertheless, although the Chartists were strongly in support of the Canadian rising and of the Irish agitation against the Act of Union, their own programme for change sought to take the same route to a share in law-making and social power as that taken successfully by the middle classes who had been admitted to the parliamentary system by the granting of the franchise in 1832. The Chartist demands were for universal (male) adult suffrage protected by the ballot and the abolition of property qualifications. Their rhetoric did not exclude a resort to arms, as the slogan 'The Charter, peaceably if we may, forcibly if we must' indicates, but their main weapons were the display of numbers in demonstrations and signatures to the petitions, backed in some areas by a degree of civil disobedience.

The Chartist narrative has been told in a number of places. Historians have had access to an enormous quantity of published material. Chartist publications in the form of journals, pamphlets and broadsides, nationally or locally produced and distributed, have survived in considerable numbers. The national and local newspaper press, which was getting off the ground during the Chartist decades, published reports and comments. Parliamentary debates and blue books, the correspondence of ministers and civil servants, memories and reminiscences of Chartists and ex-Chartists and of some of those who helped to restrain the movement as well as a well-known group of 'condition of England' novels - grouped together by critics under a phrase coined by Thomas Carlyle in his 1839 pamphlet on Chartism - combine to make Chartism one of the best-documented popular movements in history.

The mass of published words is not, however, complemented by very much in the way of visual or graphic representation of the movement or its members. Chartist publications were too early to take advantage of developments in graphic and pictorial representation which were to be brought about later in the century by advances in photographic techniques and in cheap forms of metal engraving. The most famous wood engraver of the time was a Chartist, William James Linton, but the Chartist journals printed very few wood or metal engravings and Linton did not use his engraving skills even in the journals like *The English Republic* with which he was closely associated. The most popular illustrated journal, the *Illustrated London News*, one of the first to capitalise on the new techniques of metal engraving, published a number of prints of dramatic or newsworthy events in 1842 and 1848 and these give us some idea of the appearance of aspects of Chartist actions, but there are not many of them. [Figs. 47-52 + 68 - 70] Although, therefore, we have a great many descriptions in words of Chartists and of their meetings and demonstrations, some based on experience, others on imagination, we have very few visual or graphic images to supplement the words on the page. [2]

What we have tried to do in this book is to collect together the most interesting among those examples which have survived and to offer what evidence we have of what Chartism and the Chartists actually looked like. Where must we look for Chartist pictures? Photography was in its early stages and was rarely available for the poorer members of society. Outdoor photographs were rare and there seems to have been only one Chartist demonstration which was captured by the camera, the 1848 rally on Kennington Common [figs 66-67]. There are some studio photographs of

Chartists taken in later life, but no examples of unposed photographs. Since the majority of the Chartists, including most of the local and national leaders, were working men and women, very few have left painted portraits or sculptured likenesses, with the exception of the painting of John Skevington, the Loughborough Chartist, [fig 15] and the statue of Feargus O'Connor in the Arboretum at Nottingham. One or two medallions were made, including one with a portrait to celebrate the release of Feargus O'Connor from prison in 1841, one of which was worn by the Manchester Chartist, W.H.Chadwick, until his death in 1908. [Fig 35-36]. We do, however, have a number of engravings of Chartist leaders. Portraits, some of which were used by R.G.Gammage in his history of the movement, were given away with copies of O'Connor's newspaper, the *Northern Star*, or were sold by newsagents for a shilling each. These were the portraits that hung on the walls of Chartist cottages and workrooms. W.E.Adams recalled that his grandmother and aunts, ardent Chartists all, worked as washerwomen in a room on whose wall hung a portrait of John Frost, his head surmounted by a wreath of laurel. [3] Ben Turner described in his autobiography taking down a printed almanac from the kitchen in his parents' house later in the century and finding an engraving of Ernest Jones underneath. [4] A considerable number of these prints, especially of the better-known leaders, seem to have survived. They all have in common an air of seriousness and respectability. They represent the leaders of a movement which is demanding access to the law-making processes and are the future Chartist front bench in the House of Commons. All the men wear dark suits and are either holding documents, sitting or standing beside a document-laden table, or in a few cases are posed in oratorical attitudes. This was clearly a form in which the Chartists wanted their image to be presented. No portrait here of Benjamin Rushton, the Halifax Chartist leader, variously described as a 'venerable leader of radicalism' or 'a bald-headed old rascal' according to the politics of the papers concerned, who preached bareheaded on the hillside wearing clogs and the brat or apron which was the working dress of a handloom weaver. The engravings of the Conventions and the large triptich made up of a picture of the procession accompanying the 1842 petition to Parliament, flanked on the left by a picture of Thomas Slingsby Duncombe presenting the petition in the House of Commons and on the right a picture of the 1842 convention in session, an item which is unfortunately too big to include in the present selection, are of the same type as the portraits.

There were still examples around in the 1830s of the earlier type of more expensive print, sold individually in print shops. Few of these are concerned with Chartism, although the 'ultra-radical' [fig 4] could be taken as a prototype of one representation of a Chartist in literature and in the comic papers, while the anti-Tory Poor Law print [fig 5] represents a kind of humanitarian concern with the poor which some Chartists saw as support for their cause, as indeed they appeared also to have regarded some of the work of Charles Kingsley and Elizabeth Gaskell, neither of whom in fact supported the Chartist programme.

Apart from the *Northern Star* prints, two other sets of pictures of leading Chartists were published. The first of these was a series of rather skilful line drawings of delegates to the first Convention in early 1839, published in the weekly journal *The Charter*. These are mostly profiles, heads only, drawn from life at sittings arranged between meetings [figs 16-20 & 22-24]. The second was another series published in *Reynolds's Political Instructor* in 1850. These again are skillfully drawn, heads only, in this case usually full face, and the series includes a number of leaders from the later period who were not in the earlier set [figs 56-59]. These drawings and the larger engravings are probably as near as we shall ever get to likenesses of individual Chartists. To our knowledge, no sketches or informal drawings have survived, with the exception of a doodled drawing by one of the jurors at the Special Commission at Newport in 1840 of the depressed figure of a Chartist in the dock [fig 33] [5] and a newspaper sketch of Thomas Cooper in the dock in 1842 [fig 45].

If the Chartists themselves wished to project an image of seriousness and respectability, there were plenty of people to contest them. Political cartoons were in vogue in a number of journals and working-men politicians could be fair game. A parallel could be drawn here with the treatment of Chartism in the novels of Kingsley, Gaskell, Solly and Disraeli. In all cases there is a large degree of sympathy with the aims of the Chartists, but underlying this is the fear that Chartist demands will unleash dark and violent forces among the manufacturing workers which the intelligent and sincere among the workmen will be unable to restrain. These dark forces, and the middle or upper class demagogues who appeal to them, are seen as enemies, from whose company the dignified and serious Chartist workman must be won away.

The political and satirical journals, however, operated at a rather lower level than the serious writers. Most were comparative newcomers and many of the editors and contributors were themselves radicals, even Chartist sympathisers. *Punch* had not really begun the search for establishment approval that it was to make later in the century. Feargus O'Connor was a contributor and a friend of many of the group surrounding the journal. There is not, therefore, a consistently hostile or derogatory picture to be found of the Chartists, while some of the less well-known comic journals such as *Cleave's Weekly Gazette and Satirist* were run by Chartists or ex-Chartists and were much more likely to present satirical pictures of the royal family or the leading statesmen of the day than of the Chartists. *Punch* made some kind of graphic comment on most aspects of British politics during Queen Victoria's reign, and Chartism was no exception but its view of the underside of the movement was more likely to be comic that fearful. Women Chartists were an obvious target, and *Punch's* heavy humour on the subject serves to remind us that the Chartists were in advance of most political organisations of the time in their inclusion of women as members. But in 1848, when the more romantic and middle-class revolutions of continental Europe had undoubtedly gained the sympathy of some of the editors and contributors, *Punch* for a moment held its horses. The first representation of the 1848 petition was that of a robust artisan boldly offering a massive petition to a cowering Lord John Russell [fig 71]. The comic characters in the cartoons at this time were more likely to be special constables than Chartists. Only after the dispersal of the April 10 demonstration, and the assertion that the petition contained far fewer than the numbers it claimed and a good many forgeries, did they publish the cartoon of the comic revolutionary - and also the splendid one of Colonel Sibthorp, the most reactionary and pompous Conservative member of the House, hearing that is name was among the forged signatures [figs 72-73] [6]. There is less hostility to be found in the pictures than in the writing, but the division between the serious and striving workman and the absurd or utopian uneducated follower is to be found in both.

The portrait of the leaders and the massive numbers who turned out at demonstrations and processions emphasised the Chartists' assertion of continuity with the reforming traditions of 1832. But in their representation of themselves on the membership card of the National Charter Association, founded in 1841, a different tradition can be seen [fig 34]. In the central panel the British lion appears, much as he had done in popular cartoons in the eighteenth century. He is snapping his chains and spurning the cannon and military paraphernalia around him. Above him is a globe, a cap of liberty and a tricoleur flag and on either side stand the Chartists - the man on the left with his spade and the woman on the right with a hay rake. Above them are a sheaf of corn and a beehive, below the slogan *God Is Our Guide* and the symbols of the rose, the thistle and the shamrock. The images on the card invoke another tradition - the communitarian and the agrarian which were essential elements in Chartism, although they have usually been played down or overlooked by historians.

Letters, papers and artefacts belonging to poor people rarely survive, and after 150 years we have very few Chartist items apart from prints. Perhaps the most interesting non-graphic mementoes are those connected with the Land Company. Throughout the country memories of the colonies persist, and although most of the cottages and schools have been added to, modernised or replaced, a few remain in more or less their original condition. One of these has been bought be the National Trust and is being restored as nearly as possible to its original state. The solidity and space of the Land Company cottages compare very favourably with most labourers' dwellings of the mid-nineteenth century. A unique survival - an artefact specifically created in the Chartist community - is the sampler made by ten-year-old Ann Dawson at the Heronsgate settlement. Its vivid colours and occasionally phonetic spelling bring back a sudden reminder of the movement and its optimism.

[1] David J. V. Jones *The Last Rising. The Newport Insurrection of 1839* (Oxford, 1985.)

[2] For one of the few discussions of radical, including Chartist, iconography, see James Epstein, 'Understanding the Cap of Liberty' in *Past and Present* no. 122 (Feb 1989)

[3] W.E.Adams, *Memoirs of a Social Atom* (London 1903)

[4] Ben Turner, *About Myself* (London 1930)

[5] Reproduced in Keith Kissack, *Victorian Monmouth*, (Ledbury, n.d.

1980?) We are grateful to Councillor Jeff Carpenter of Worcester for drawing our attention to this item

[6] We are grateful to Edward Royle for pointing out the importance of the dating of these cartoons

ACKNOWLEDGEMENTS

We are neither of us art historians and offer the pictures in this volume as a contribution to Social History rather than to Art History. We have been given help in putting the collection together by a large number of people. For their acts of assistance we are grateful to Owen Ashton, Jeff Carpenter, Ian Foster, Robert Fyson, Brian Harrison, Peter James, Alain Kahan, Angela Killick, Alice Lock, Brian Maidment, Edward Royle, Barrie Trinder and Alan Yates. Martin Eve of Merlin Press has supported the project with scholarship and patience.

We are grateful to the proprietors of the journals concerned for permission to reproduce items from the *Illustrated London News* and *Punch*, and to Her Majesty the Queen for permission to include the photographs (figs 66-67) which are in the Royal Archives at Windsor Castle.

Our thanks are due to the staff of the following institutions for their help with our searches: Birmingham Central Library; the Bodleian Library, Oxford; the British Library; Dudley Archives; Halifax Central Library; Huddersfield Central Library; Leicester City Museums; the National Library of Wales; the National Museum of Labour History; the National Portrait Gallery; Newcastle-upon-Tyne Central Library; Newport Central Library; Paisley Central Library; Tameside Local Studies Library; Tullie House Museum and Art Gallery, Carlisle; and the Working Class Movement Library, Salford.

Every effort has been made to obtain the necessary permissions to use the material included in this book. If anyone has been overlooked, please will they get in touch with the editors through Merlin Press.

LIST OF PLATES

Plates 66 and 67 are from the Royal Archives, by gracious permission of Her Majesty the Queen.

Plates 6, 7, 10, 29 and 30 appear by courtesy of the National Portrait Gallery, London.

Plates 8, 47, 48, 49, 50, 51, 52, 64, 65, 68, 69 and 70 are taken from *the Illustrated London News,* by permission of the proprietors.

Plates 39, 40, 41, 71, 72, 73 and 74 are from *Punch*, by permission of Punch Ltd.

Plates 16, 17, 18, 19, 20, 22, 23 and 24 are from *The Charter* (1839) by courtesy of the Birmingham Library Services.

Plates 31 and 32 appear by courtesy of the National Library of Wales

Plates 42 and 55 by courtesy of the Bodleian Library Oxford

Plates 2, 3, 4, 5, 11, 21, 27, 43, 60 and 76 from the collection of Dorothy Thompson

The sampler on the cover of the book is in the possession of Angela Killick and appears with her permission

1. The Four Factions which distract the Country   The Whig

2. The Four Factions which distract the Country   The Tory

3. The Four Factions which distract the Country   The Liberal

4. The Four Factions which distract the Country   The Ultra Radical

23. Robert Knox

24. Robert Lowery

25. Henry Vincent [collection of Barry Trinder]

26. The Attack of the Chartists on the Westgate Hotel [collection of Stephen Roberts]

27. The Westgate Hotel after the Chartist Attack

28. John Frost

29. John Frost during his trial

30. John Frost, condemned to death for High Treason

31. Zephaniah Williams

32. William Jones

33. Drawing of Chartists in dock [from K. Kissack, *Victorian Monmouth* (Ledbury n.d.)]

34. Membership card of the National Charter Association [from A. Marcroft (ed) *Landmarks of Local Liberalism* (1913)]

35. Medal struck to commemorate the release of O'Connor from York Castle in August 1841 [by courtesy Tullie House Museum and Art Gallery, Carlisle]

36. Medal struck to commemorate the release of O'Connor from York Castle in August 1841 [by courtesy Tullie House Museum and Art Gallery, Carlisle]

55. William Thom [from *The Illuminated Magazine* 1844, by courtesy of the Bodleian Library, University of Oxford, Shelfmark Per 2705 d.28]

56. George Julian Harney

57. Edmund Stallwood

58. Philip McGrath

59. William Cuffay

60. Patrick O'Higgins

61. Martin Jude

62. Feargus O'Connor and the Land Plan

63. Thomas Merrick and Philip Ford, allottees [from Alice Mary Hadfield, *The Chartist Land Company* (Newton Abbot, 1970)]

64. Snig's End Estate

65. Cottages at Snig's End

66. Kennington Common, April 10, 1848

67. Kennington Common, April 10, 1848

68. Chartist Procession 1848

69. The Chartist Convention 1848

70. Police at the Chartist meeting 1848

71. Not so *very* unreasonable, eh?

72. A Physical Force Chartist

73. Colonel Sibthorp

74. A Special Constable dries his gunpowder

75. Four-warned, Four-armed [Mary Evans Picture Library]

76. Ernest Jones

77. Samuel Kydd

78. John Bedford Leno

79. W.H. Chadwick [from T. Palmer Newbould *Pages From a Life of Strife. Being Some Recollections of William Henry Chadwick, the last of the Manchester Chartists (1911)* by courtesy of the Manchester Central Library]

80. The Old Chartist

INTRODUCTION

There are a great many books on Chartism, most of which have very little in the way of illustrations. This is a book which is almost all illustrations and very little in the way of text. A brief account of the movement with captions giving extra information about the subjects of the pictures can provide only a skeletal outline of events which filled two decades and more. The short list of further reading at the end suggests guides to a fuller narrative and to the consideration of some of the alternative interpretations of the story and lists bibliographies in which all the existing writing about all aspects of Chartism is to be found.

The Chartist movement got its name from the document known as the People's Charter, first published in May 1838. This was in the form of a petition to Parliament calling for six reforming measures to widen the franchise to include all adult male citizens of sane mind and untainted by crime, and to make each vote cast of approximately equal value. The Charter arose directly from the agitation which had brought in the a series of basic reforms to the British Parliamentary system in the late 1820s and early 1830s. Outstanding among these measures were the repeal of the Test and Corporation Acts of 1828 which gave political and other civic rights to Protestant non-conformists, the 1829 Catholic Emancipation Act which admitted Catholics to public office and, above all, the 1832 Reform Act which reorganised the parliamentary constituencies of Britain to allow for the great demographic changes of the early industrial period and which granted the suffrage in the boroughs to holders of property other than land. Extra-Parliamentary pressure had contributed largely to the achievement of these reforms and the Chartists hoped and believed that an extension of such pressure could continue the reforming process to include those whose only property lay in their labour, The six points were to be the extension of the franchise to all male citizens, a secret ballot and equal electoral districts to protect the vote, the abolition of the property qualification for would-be members of the House of Commons - a qualification which required in 1838 a considerable income from freehold property - the payment of Members of Parliament and annual elections at which members would report back to their constituencies and offer themselves for re-election. All these points, except the final one, were to become part of the system during the century after the movement ended.

The method by which the campaign for the Charter was to be waged was the traditional one open to non-electors, the petition to Parliament. This was, however, to be a new kind of petition, organised on a national scale with signatures coming from every part of the kingdom and backed up by mass meetings, often held simultaneously in various parts of the country and by a General Convention or anti-parliament elected by universal open votes at these mass meetings. The Convention was to debate tactics, to spread the message of the movement and to supervise the presentation of the petition. The aim of the Chartists was not to overthrow the existing institutions of government but to widen them to admit all citizens to the law-making process. The suffrage for women was not one of the six points, and it was by no means universally advocated in the movement, It was nevertheless strongly supported especially in the textile manufacturing districts where women played an essential part in the movement.

Apart from the General Convention and indoor and outdoor meetings, the Chartist movement produced printed material of all kinds, from handbills and broadsides to the most widely-circulated provincial newspaper in the country, the weekly *Northern Star,* owned and published from Leeds by Feargus O'Connor, the foremost national leader of the movement. The *Star* was founded in the autumn of 1837 and may be seen, with the publication of the Charter soon after, as the starting point of the movement. The reporting of the *Star* and the circulation of the National Petition gathered together those who had been active in the various earlier agitations for parliamentary reform and for other issues such as factory reform, press freedom and above all the movements of opposition to the 1834 Poor Law Amendment Act. Large numbers of new younger supporters joined the veteran reformers in a movement which swept the country.

Although the aim of the movement was the peaceful achievement of the reforms contained in its programme, there were many Chartists who believed that they would be forced to resort to arms either to defend the working people against increased government repression which appeared to be under consideration at the end of the thirties and for which there were plenty of models in continental Europe, or to force through their programme if all peaceful means of petition failed. The one significant armed rising which was attempted took place in Wales in the autumn of 1839 at a point at which the authorities had begun to round up and arrest local and national Chartist leaders throughout the country after the rejection of the first petition.

In early November 1839 thousands of armed men marched on the South Welsh town of Newport. Their plans were not fully coordinated and appalling weather delayed and impeded the marchers. A brief engagement with a small detachment of soldiers based in the Westgate Hotel at Newport forced the Chartists to retreat, leaving twenty-two dead. In the weeks that followed known leaders were rounded up and early in 1840 tried by a Special Commission sent in to the district. Sentence of death was passed on the three chief leaders, John Frost, a former magistrate of the town and a prominent leader of the local and of the national movement, Zephaniah Williams and William Jones.

Petitions and meetings demanding clemency were held throughout the country and there can be little doubt that the authorities' prompt action in commuting the sentences as well as the widespread practice in the local courts of releasing arrested Chartists without sending them to trial helped to defuse an extremely tense situation.

The events of 1839 undoubtedly alarmed some sympathetic middle-class supporters of Chartism by raising the spectre of uncontrolled violence. They also reinforced the belief in the power of petitioning since it was widely believed that the massive petitions for clemency, which exceeded in the number of signatures those of the Charter itself, had affected the government's decision. They also, of course, demonstrated the great difficulty of bringing even armed civilians into conflict with trained military personnel.

The petition was presented to Parliament twice more, in 1842 and in 1848. Both these years were years of considerable industrial disturbance. The summer of 1842 probably saw more people on the streets in protest against wage reductions and demanding political reform than any other time in the century. There were strikes and lock-outs in the mining district of the Black Country, which rapidly spread throughout the Potteries, and in Yorkshire and Lancashire, where the so-called 'plug riots' saw parties of striking or locked-out operatives pull the plugs of the boilers in the mills to enforce stoppage and call out all the workpeople. Because much of the 1842 activity was in the form of strikes and lock-outs and occurred in the textile

17

manufacturing and mining districts some historians have suggested that there were two forms of action occurring - the industrial which related to wages and was spontaneous and non-political and the political or Chartist. Although there was undoubtedly some disagreement among the Chartist leaders as to how far they should go with the turn-outs and protesters, the evidence clearly shows that for the people on the streets there was no division between the industrial and the political. There were attempts made during some of the subsequent trials of the leaders to emphasise the provocation given by wage-cuts at a time of recession and poverty, but observers of all kinds agreed on the interaction of the language of politics and Chartism with that of industrial militancy.

The 1842 petition is an interesting document. The petition asks for the petitioners to be allowed to present their arguments for the six points at the bar of the House. In the preamble to the central six points the petition brings up a series of issues which the existing House of Commons has failed to address, but which a House elected by 'the whole people' would have dealt with. As well as the need to extend the suffrage beyond the small minority of the population who enjoy it, the preamble points to the great inequalities of numbers between different constituencies, the great amount of bribery, intimidation and corruption taking place at elections, the heavy taxation being exacted to pay for unjust wars in the past, taxes imposed contrary to the provisions of the Bill of Rights, the punishment of poverty and old age by the draconian provisions of the new Poor Law, the contrast between the daily allowance given to Queen Victoria, Prince Albert and other members of the royal family and the twopence or threepence on which 'thousands of the tax payers of this empire' were expected to live, the infringement of the right of peaceful assembly by the arrest and imprisonment of speakers at outdoor meetings, the growth of 'an unconstitutional police force' throughout the county 'to prevent the due exercise of the people's rights', the existence of an unconstitutional standing army, the overlong hours of labour, especially in the factories, the starvation wages of agricultural labourers, the taxation of food and other necessities and the existence of monopolies by the few of 'the suffrage, of paper money, of machinery, of land, of the public press and of a host of other evils all arising from class legislation which your Honourable House has always consistently endeavoured to maintain instead of diminish'. Further objection is raised to the maintenance and the great cost of a Church

Establishment and an expensive bench of Bishops, a protest is made against the sentences on Frost, Williams and Jones and a call for the repeal of the Act of Union with Ireland. Social and political questions appear side by side, 'your petitioners' being of the opinion that 'the Poor Law Bastille and the Police Stations, being co-existent, have originated from the same cause, viz the increased desire on the part of the *iresponsible few* to oppress and starve the many.'

In the course of the preamble it is more than once suggested that the continued denial of the rights of citizenship will lead to outbreaks of violence, but it is nowhere suggested that the institutions of government should be swept away, only that they should be reformed and widened to include 'the whole people'.

The third presentation of the petition took place on the tenth of April 1848. There had been meetings of the Convention between 1842 and 1848 and preparations had been begun in the hard winter of 1847 for a new and final petition to parliament. The French revolution of February 1848 was welcomed with great enthusiasm and meetings throughout the country put out the slogan 'France has the republic - England shall have the Charter'. In Ireland the campaign for the repeal of the union, which under the leadership of Daniel O'Connell had held aloof from cooperation with the Chartists, split and a group led by the leaders of Young Ireland called for armed action against British rule and eventually for cooperation with Chartism. The arrest and sentencing of the Irish leaders, particularly John Mitchel, help to fuel the increasingly militant campaign in parts of Britain during the summer of 1848 after the rejection of the third petition, and these months saw the arrest and imprisonment of a number of the more prominent local and national Chartist leaders.

Throughout the years in which Chartism flourished there were a series of attempts to forge an alliance between the most radical of the mainstream politicians and sections of the Chartist leadership. There is no space here to go into the story of these attempts, but it has to be seen that there were certain issues on which the more radical Whig and Liberal politicians agreed with the Chartists - including the need for a widening of the suffrage. There were other questions such as the police force and the operation of the Poor Law on which some traditionalist Tories sympathised with the working class radicals. Only a small handful of politicians, however, agreed with the whole programme of the Chartist movement and helped to present its case in Parliament. Feargus O'Connor himself was elected for Nottingham in 1847 and joined T. S. Duncombe and Thomas Wakley in the House of Commons. These two, together with John Fielden, had been the Chartists' consistent supporters from the beginning, although even Duncombe was not prepared to support the demand of the 1842 petition for the repeal of the Act of Union with Ireland.

After 1848 some Chartist organisations continued for another ten years or so. Most of the members turned away from politics towards more social movements in their own localities or trades, although the presence of many former Chartists in the campaign for the 1867 Reform Act indicated that they were still concerned with the political agenda. The Chartists' own attempt at social organisation, the National Land Company, failed financially but the five settlements that had been established in the late 1840s continued in existence, though mostly not in the hands of the original allottees. Chartists were however prominent among the founder-members of the cooperative societies, friendly and insurance societies, emigration societies and trade unions which grew up in the manufacturing districts during the third quarter of the nineteenth century. Many also took part in local government, on councils and on school boards. A large number emigrated and the labour movements in Australia and the United States record many ex-Chartists among their founders.

The chief legacies of the British Chartists were firstly the setting of the admission of working people to the suffrage firmly on the agenda, and secondly the reining in of the orgy of unrestrained action which the new industrial class had hoped would provide a free and available labour force for the expanding industries of the century. The draconian Poor Law provisions of 1834 were never fully applied and were considerably modified around the mid-century. Trade unions developed and protected apprenticeship regulation at least among the skilled trades, police forces were introduced slowly and based on local initiatives rather than the brasher national forces which early advocates of skilled policing had advocated. Perhaps, above all, the movement gave confidence in the power of mass public opinion and in some cases experience of administration which were fed into the organisations which began to form a new labour movement in the later years of the century.

THE IMAGES

THE FOUR FACTIONS WHICH DISTRACT THE COUNTRY

A cartoon of the period between the Reform Bill and the publication of the People's Charter. This view of the Ultra Radical is very much the way in which the Chartists were to be presented by their opponents.

1. WHIG
'Place, plunder, hypocrisy and deceit' - Grey in the Cause

Self is the first love of nature, particularly in these awful and uncertain times, and nobody has ever accused me and my party of its violation, since we've been in the public service. *I find my influence drawing pretty fast to a close, and of course it now behoves me to look out for the* future *comforts of myself, my brothers, sisters, nephews, sons in law, uncles, aunts and a regiment of poor cousins &c, &c, &c*
[On the placard in his hand - *I have only got £137,000 per Annum for myself and family*]

2. TORY
'Bullets, bayonets, blood, barbarity and fire'

I must begin to sharp my knife and get ready for place, for I expect to get reinstated soon in my old station as master man butcher, *at the head of the nation's affairs *. Must begin to get all the slaughter houses into good order (i.e. bastilles, county gaols and police station houses) expects rare sticking amongst the* lambs. My dog'll *hunt 'em down and we Tories 'll* finish *'em.*
* our conservative plot is going on famously*

3. LIBERAL

A sort of go-between, neither for us or against us, but all for himself, in short a rank coward.

'Church and King, obedience to the laws, however unjust, and non-resistance'

Oh crikey, there'll be a rumpus I know soon. Vell, arter all there's nothing like good order, and taking everything quiet; for an't ve taught to 'forgive them that trespass against us'? Vy, if a man should happen to shuv his hand into vun's pocket, ve should try to convince him of the vickedness of it, and if he should happen to clap a pistol to vun's head, vy then vun ought to take the law of him, and if it should happen to go off before that, vy then of course the law will take its course. *Oh jemmeny if there ant guns a going off in the street; however this is a jolly good hiding place up here. Oh I'm blest if they ant a coming upstairs, - oh, murder, help.*

4. ULTRA RADICAL

*That is, not a true and honest Radical, but a scum of the rabble, a ragamuffin
ruffian, everything to gain and nothing to lose
'Anarchy, confusion, robbery and death to all who differ from us'*

*My eyes, how I longs for a riverlution. Jest to see all Lunnon in a blaze, and all
the rich kiddies hanging on lamp posts. Oh strike me lucky, vouldn't ve rifle all the
shops, break open all the prisons, and let out all the thieves to help us. Vot a lark.
That are's vot I call 'liberty'*

Sir Robert, I have taken the liberty of calling on you,
before you leave Town, to beg you will do something for
my starving family; it is a case of urgent necessity
and I hope you will not refuse!

Mr Bull, this is a most unreasonable time for such an application, dont you know that Pheasant Shooting has commenced, and Hunting is just beginning? All Parliamentary business is at an end for the present, but if you will call on me in a few months (its a short time to wait) I will give your case mature consideration, and in a couple of years from that time, if necessary, I will see what can be done for you.

"APPLICATION NOT GRANTED."
(A term generally used at the different Boards of Guardians when the poor apply for relief.)

5. The Poor Law Amendment Act of 1834 made relief for the able-bodied available only in workhouses, where families were split up. It was opposed by some paternalist Tories and other humanitarians, as well as by working class radicals. The sympathy of their betters on this issue was sometimes mistaken for sympathy with Chartism.

FEARGUS O'CONNOR, ESQ.ʳ

6. Feargus O'Connor (1794-1855). Gentleman-orator and owner of the *Northern Star*, O'Connor was a charismatic and immensely popular leader. A prisoner in York castle for fifteen months in 1840-1, his release was celebrated in the lines of Thomas Cooper, 'The lion of freedom comes from his den/we'll rally around him again and again ...'

James Bronterre O'Brien

7. James Bronterre O'Brien (1804-1864). Writing under the name of Bronterre, he became one of the most powerful and influential radical journalists of the pre-Chartist period, Editor of *The Poor Man's Guardian* and other journals, he initially cooperated with the Chartist leaders and wrote powerful columns in the *Northern Star*. After 1842 he quarrelled with O'Connor and for a time joined one of the middle-class radical movements. He remained a radical until his death, leaving a legacy of followers, particularly in the radical debating clubs of the metropolis.

8. Feargus O'Connor presented in a non-Chartist journal. Historians have too often accepted the view of him as simply a powerful demagogue. In fact his newspaper held the movement together, he was responsible for setting up the National Charter Association in 1840, the first national membership-based political organisation in Britain, and for founding the National Land Company in 1845. Whatever view may be taken of his politics, he clearly possessed political talents as well as the gift of oratory.
Illustrated London News 8 October 1842

9. Joseph Rayner Stephens (1805-1879). A former Methodist minister, Stephens formed his own radical congregation, amongst whom he campaigned against the 'unchristian and unconstitutional' New Poor Law. His arrest in December 1838 was seen by his extensive following as the beginning of a government reign of terror. His initial support for Chartism waned after his eighteen months' imprisonment, although he remained a radical all his life, opposing among other things the temperance movement and any attack on the traditional ale houses.

10. William Lovett (1800 - 1877). His part in drawing up the People's Charter and his later autobiography, with its denunciations of O'Connor, have given Lovett a more prominent place in the history of Chartism than he probably deserves. He never joined the National Charter Association, and after 1841 was only associated with radical initiatives peripheral to mainstream Chartism.

11. John Collins (1802 - 1852). A fellow prisoner with Lovett at Warwick, Collins came from Birmingham and, highly regarded locally, became a town councillor in 1847.

THE TREE OF TAXATION.

12. Among the full-sized Chartist newspapers one of the most impressive and successful was the *Northern Liberator*, published in Newcastle-on-Tyne and edited during the early years of Chartism by a talented group of young journalists which included the Irishman Thomas Ainge Devyr. This cartoon illustrates the basis of the paper's message.
Northern Liberator, 13 October 1838.

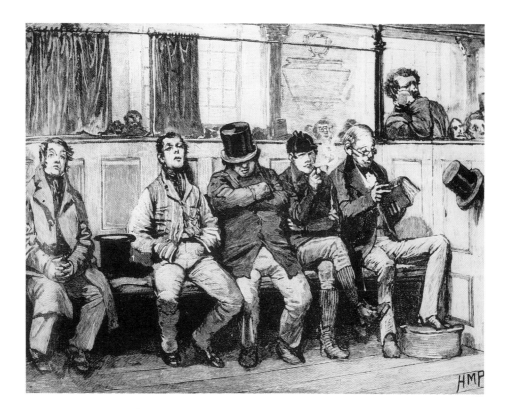

13. A sit-in by Chartists in a church. A form of demonstration widely used during the early years of the movement was the invasion of parish churches. A crowd of Chartist members would take their seats in pews for which they had not paid pew-rent and often demand that the sermon be preached from one of their favourite texts. In this case they are dressed informally, wearing hats and smoking - behaviour totally out of place in church.

14. The General Convention of 1839. It was pressing on the borderline of legality to organise a Convention, and the Chartists were careful never to refer to a 'national' convention. The delegates who assembled at the British Hotel in Charing Cross early in February 1839 were a deliberately respectable selection, a number of whom withdrew when the tone of the debates became confrontational. The Convention sent out speakers, known as missionaries, to spread the message throughout the country. In May it moved to Birmingham which was seen as a more radical base than London. The first petition was presented to Parliament - and rejected - in July.

15. John Skevington (1801 - 1850). Representative of the men who formed local Chartist leadership, Skevington of Loughborough had been a boy preacher in the Primitive Methodist connection and later an Owenite. He was a hatter by trade and the main organiser of the Loughborough Chartists.

PORTRAITS OF DELEGATES.
No. XII.

JOHN SKEVINGTON.

16. John Skevington. *The Charter*, 19 May 1839.

PORTRAITS OF DELEGATES.
No. VIII.

THOMAS RAYNER SMART.

17. Another Loughborough delegate, Smart was by trade a carpenter and was also a schoolmaster and a poet. He was proud to claim an ancestor who had fought under Cromwell.
The Charter, 21 April 1839.

PORTRAITS OF DELEGATES.
No. XI.

HENRY HETHERINGTON.

18. Henry Hetherington (1792 - 1849). Publisher of the *Poor Man's Guardian*, indomitable campaigner against the 'taxes on knowledge' and signatory of the People's Charter in 1838, Hetherington died of cholera, in spite of his belief that being a vegetarian protected him from the disease. *The Charter*, 12 May 1839.

PORTRAITS OF DELEGATES.
No. V.

MATTHEW FLETCHER.

19. Matthew Fletcher (1795 - 1878). A surgeon from Bury in Lancashire, Fletcher was a passionate opponent of the 1834 Poor Law and initially joined the campaign of the Chartists, believing that Universal Suffrage would be the best protection against the policies of the 'reforming' Liberals. He was never easy with extreme radicalism, however, and withdrew from Chartism in its later years.
The Charter, 31 March 1839

PORTRAITS OF DELEGATES.

No. VI.

PETER M. M'DOUALL.

20. Peter Murray McDouall (1814 - 1854[?]). A surgeon by profession, McDouall became a radical through his work among the handloom weavers. He remained a leading Chartist throughout his short life, published letters and journals and served two terms of imprisonment. He was top of the poll for the executive of the National Charter Association in 1841 and 1842 and again in 1848.

The Charter, 7 April 1839

21. The *Northern Star* engraving of McDouall

PORTRAITS OF DELEGATES.
No. X.

PETER BUSSEY.

22. Peter Bussey of Bradford. A leading West Riding radical, who had been involved in all the campaigns which preceded Chartism during the 1830s, including the putting up of a universal suffrage candidate in the first election after the Reform Act. Originally a merchant in the textile trade, he became, like many local Chartist leaders, owner of a beerhouse which became a centre for radical meetings and the place to which convention delegates reported back. He was almost certainly involved in illegal insurrectionary planning in early 1840 and fled to America after the arrest of the Welsh leaders. *The Charter*, 5 May 1839

PORTRAITS OF DELEGATES.
No. IV.

ROBERT KNOX.

23. Robert Knox. A slater from Duns, Knox was a prominent
Sunderland Chartist until his marriage in 1840. *The Charter*,
24 March 1839.

PORTRAITS OF DELEGATES.
No. IX.

ROBERT LOWERY.

24. Robert Lowery (1809 - 1863). One of the outstanding orators among the younger Chartists, Lowery was a popular missionary in the early years of the movement. He later withdrew from Chartism and used his oratorical powers to support the temperance movement. *The Charter*, 28 April 1839

25. Henry Vincent (1813-1878). A popular early Chartist lecturer, Vincent embraced temperance and, in due course, an alliance with middle class reformers. He married the daughter of the radical publisher, John Cleave.

The attack of the Chartists on the Westgate Hotel, Newport, Nov.: 4th 1839

26. A number of pictures survive of the events at Newport in November 1839. The second of these two was drawn by one of the soldiers who took part in the defence of the Westgate Hotel and shows the scene after the Chartists had withdrawn.

JOHN FROST.

Leader of the Chartists in Monmouthshire Nov. 4th 1839

28. John Frost (1784 - 1877). Frost who had been a radical since his earliest years, had taken an active part in reforming politics in South Wales and had been mayor of Newport and a member of the bench of magistrates in the town. He was removed from the magistracy because of his association with Chartism and was seen as one of the major national leaders, as well as the leader of the Welsh Chartists. The sentences of death passed on him and his fellow leaders of the Newport rising were commuted to transportation for life. He was finally granted leave to return to Britain in 1856.

JOHN FROST, (THE CHARTIST)

29. Frost during his trial.

MR JOHN FROST,
CONDEMNED TO DEATH FOR HIGH TREASON,
Jan.ʸ 8ᵗʰ 1840.

30. John Frost condemned to death for High Treason

CHARTIST CHIEFS
№ 2
ZEPHANIAH WILLIAMS,

31. Zephaniah Williams (1784 - 1877). Atheist radical mine agent kept an inn which was a meeting place for radicals of all kinds. In Van Dieman's land after his transportation he recognised coal-bearing country and became a wealthy mine owner there in his later years.

JONES, THE WATCHMAKER.

32. William Jones (1809 - 1873). The third of the transported Welsh leaders failed to make a life for himself in Australia and died there in poverty in 1873.

33. Drawing by J. E. W. Rolls, a member of the Grand Jury at the Special Commission in Monmouth in January 1840 of one of the Welsh Chartists in the dock. Note the figures of Frost, Williams and Jones hanging from the gallows in the background.

CHARTISTS' MEMBERSHIP CARD.
Lent by Councillor James K. Cheetham, the Liberal Agent. It was his grand-
father's membership card.

34. Membership card for the National Charter Association. Founded in July 1840, the NCA provided a means of local organisation for the Chartists and offered leadership and the sense of belonging to a national movement. It was pressing on the borders of legality to establish a national body with local branches at this time.

35. Feargus O'Connor Liberation Medal, 1841. When Chartist leaders were released from prison there were processions, public teas and lecture tours, and no more so than when O'Connor emerged from York Castle in August 1841.

36. The rear of the medal, depicting Feargus' place of incarceration

37. Thomas Slingsby Duncombe M.P. (1790 - 1867). Duncombe
came from a wealthy landowning background, son of Thomas
Duncombe Esq. of Duncombe Park, Yorkshire and nephew of Lord
Faversham. He was member for Finsbury in North London and with
his fellow-member, Thomas Wakley, was a consistent supporter of all
aspects of the Chartist programme except the repeal of the Union. He
was described by Friedrich Engels as 'the voice of Labour' in
Parliament. He was the only Member of Parliament apart from
O'Connor to hold a membership card of the National Charter
Association.

38. The procession and petition of 1842. The petition was signed by 3,317,752 working people. Pasted together and folded by members of the Chartist Convention, it was carried, in a large wooden frame and with great difficulty, by relays of thirty men to the House of Commons.

39. Mary Ann Walker. A Chartist lecturer and writer, a member of the City of London Female Chartist Association. *Punch* always found the idea of women Chartists hilarious and there is no reason to suppose that this caricature bears any resemblance to its subject.
Punch 1842, vol.2

THE MODERN MILO.

40. Feargus O'Connor as Milo, the athlete of ancient times, who was said to have tried to uproot a tree which, when half-cleft, reunited and trapped his hands, allowing him to be eaten by wild beasts. *Punch* 1842, vol.2

HOW TO TREAT THE FEMALE CHARTISTS.

41. For *Punch* the existence of female Chartists was an opportunity that could not be missed.
Punch, 1848, vol. 8

42. Robert Kemp Philp (1819 - 1892). A supporter of joint action with middle class politicians, Philp was one of a number of Bath Chartists who defected to the Complete Suffrage movement in 1842. He later became a compiler of a series of practical handbooks, including *Enquire Within Upon Everything* (1856), which, in thirty years, sold one million copies. *The Family Treasury*, 1853-4.

43. William Prowting Roberts (1806 - 1871). A solicitor who gave consistent support to Chartists and trade unionists and who near the end of his life worked with Ernest Jones to defend the Manchester Fenians, Roberts was a close friend of O'Connor and helped to launch and promote the Land Company. His work amongst the miners earned him the nickname of 'the Miners' Attorney General'.

THOMAS COOPER,
AUTHOR OF "THE PURGATORY OF SUICIDES."

DRAWN BY H. ANELAY; ENGRAVED BY H. LINTON.

44. Thomas Cooper (1805 - 1892). 'General' of the Shakespearean Association of Leicester Chartists, Cooper spent two years in prison after the outbreak in the Potteries. There he wrote a lengthy poem, *The Purgatory of Suicides* (1845), and subsequently published verse, fiction and journalism. His autobiography (1872) is one of the most vivid works of Chartist recollection. He lived to a considerable age, writing and lecturing on Christian subjects in the later part of his life. *Howitt's Journal* 1848, vol. 3

We present our readers with a slight

SKETCH OF COOPER,

AS HE APPEARED AT THE BAR.

45. Cooper at his first trial. He faced a charge of arson, but was acquitted; five months later he was found guilty of seditious conspiracy. *North Staffordshire Mercury*, 15 October 1842.

46. Jeremiah Yates (1810 - 1852). A Chartist newsagent and potter, Yates was imprisoned for twelve months after the 1842 riots in the Potteries.

47. Popular violence in the Potteries during the 1842 general strike for the Charter. *Illustrated London News*, 22 October 1842

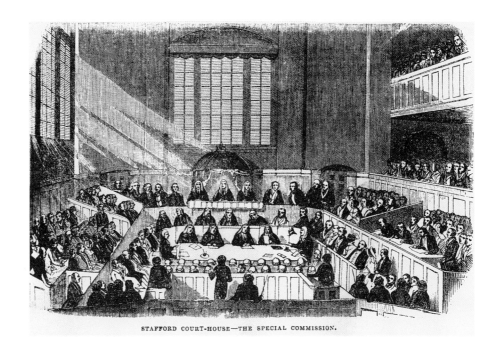

STAFFORD COURT-HOUSE—THE SPECIAL COMMISSION.

48. The Special Commission of the Assize which met after the riots in the Potteries. In just two weeks the Special Commission dealt with 276 people, sentencing fifty-six of them to transportation. It was the largest Chartist trial ever held. *Illustrated London News*, 22 October 1842

49. The general strike in Manchester. More force was thrown against the authorities in 1842 than in any other year in the nineteenth century. In Lancashire, as elsewhere, wage cuts began the protests. *Illustrated London News*, 20 August 1842

50. Soldiers and strikers outside a mill in Salford. *Illustrated London News*, 20 August 1842.

51. In Preston soldiers opened fire on Chartist crowds, which included women and children. *Illustrated London News*, 27 August 1842

52. In Halifax there was an attack by Chartists on soldiers who had
been escorting prisoners to the railway station. *Illustrated London
News*, 27 August 1842

SATURDAY, SEPTEMBER 3, 1842.

PRINTED AND PUBLISHED BY H. HETHERINGTON, 13 AND 14, WINE-OFFICE-COURT, FLEET-STREET, LONDON.

THE CHARTISTS ARE COMING, OH, DEAR! OH DEAR!

Oh, O! what I've caught a few of you at last, have I? Ah! It's my turn now.
Oh, pray have mercy on a poor imbecile old man. Oh, Lord, I wish I was at home at Apsley House, with Charlotte Arburthnot.
JEMMY GRAHAM. Hoot mon. I hope ye are no' going to shoot.
SPINNING BOBBY. If I get well out of this. I shall consider myself uncommon *lucky*.

53. A cartoon poking fun at the Cabinet during the crisis of 1842. *The Oddfellow*, 3 September 1842.

SATURDAY, DECEMBER 10, 1842.

LONDON :— PRINTED AND PUBLISHED BY WILLIAM JOHNSTON, LITTLE RED LION COURT, CHARTERHOUSE LANE.

LAW MAKING A MEAL IN THE MANUFACTURING DISTRICTS.

" Though your sins be as *Scarlet.*"

54. As this cartoon points out, the authorities struck back harshly after the strikes were over. *The Oddfellow*, 10 December 1842.

THOM, THE INVERURY POET.

55. William Thom (1798 - 1848). A much-loved Scottish poet, a number of whose poems have survived in anthologies. Thom lived in London in the mid-1840s, and was well known among radicals as a singer and raconteur. *The Illuminated Magazine*, IV, November 1844.

JULIAN HARNEY.

56. George Julian Harney (1817 - 1897). A prominent figure throughout the history of the movement, Harney was editor of the *Northern Star* after 1845 and a close associate of Friedrich Engels. He later lived in America but returned permanently to Britain in 1888; in his last years he wrote a number of Chartist obituaries for W. E. Adams' *Newcastle Weekly Chronicle*. *Reynolds's Political Instructor*, 16 February 1850.

57. Edmund Stallwood. A London Chartist who had been a gardener but was mainly known as a journalist, he lived for a time as a Land Company settler at Charterville, the settlement in Oxfordshire.
Reynolds's Political Instructor, 27 April 1850

58. Philip McGrath. An Irish tailor, McGrath was very popular amongst his own London Chartists. He worked closely with O'Connor, becoming a director of the Land Company.
Reynolds's Political Instructor, 20 March 1850.

MR. WILLIAM CUFFAY.

59. William Cuffay (1788 - 1870). The son of a Caribbean slave, Cuffay came to Chartism after the defeat of the London tailors' strike of 1834. He was a much-respected and trusted member of the metropolitan Chartists, and served as an auditor of the Land Company. Transported in 1848 for his part in the 'Orange Tree Conspiracy', he played an active role in Tasmanian politics until his death.
Reynolds's Political Instructor, 13 April 1850.

60. Patrick O'Higgins (1790 - 1854). O'Higgins was the best-known of the group of Chartists in Dublin. A textile merchant by trade, he had been with William Cobbett on the latter's Irish tour and was a life-long supporter of universal suffrage and opponent of the Act of Union. He was sent to prison for two years in 1848 for having firearms in his house.

61. Martin Jude (1805 - 1860). Leader of the miners in the North-east and one of the outstanding figures of nineteenth century trade unionism, Jude was a committed Chartist. Denied employment at his trade, he kept an inn and was an agent for the *Northern Star*.

62. Feargus O'Connor with Land Plan farms. The plan, started in 1845, involved the purchase by O'Connor and the executive of the Land Company of rural estates which were divided into holdings of two, three or four acres, on each of which a substantial cottage was built Members of the Plan paid a small weekly subscription and drew lots for settlements. The rent which the settlers paid went to service the mortgages on the land and to buy new land for further settlement. Five settlements were opened, but the scheme failed eventually.

63. Thomas Merrick (above) and Philip Ford, original allottees at O'Connorville near Watford, the first of the land settlements to be opened.

64. Houses at Snig's End. The cottages were spacious and well-built and many have survived, mostly with due modernisation, until the present. By the standards of their time they were excellent dwellings. *Illustrated London News,* 23 February 1850

65. Cottages at Snig's End
Illustrated London News, 23 February 1850

66. Daguerrotype of the meeting on Kennington Common, 10 April 1848.
There were probably upwards of 20,000 people present, but the fact that
Kennington was south of the River meant that the authorities and military,
by controlling the bridges over the Thames, were able to restrict the
numbers who accompanied the Petition to the House of Commons. It was
eventually transported in three cabs, accompanied by the National Charter
Association executive committee.

67. Another view of the Kennington Common meeting.

PART OF THE PROCESSION.—SKETCHED AT BLACKFRIARS-BRIDGE

68. Procession of Chartists, 10 April 1848. *Illustrated London News*, 15 April 1848.

69. The Chartist Convention of 1848. After the rejection of the petition, the Convention dispersed and the activities of the disturbed summer that followed were mostly organised in the provincial centres. One metropolitan action which led to a number of arrests and transportations was the so-called 'Orange Tree conspiracy', so named after the public house in which the conspirators met, in which Chartists and Irish nationalists were involved in planning a rising.
Illustrated London News, 15 April 1848

CHARTIST EXCITEMENT.—THE POLICE FORCE IN BONNER'S-FIELDS, ON MONDAY LAST,

70. A Chartist demonstration attended by the police. *Illustrated London News*, 17 June 1848.

NOT SO VERY UNREASONABLE!!!

71. A Bill containing the six points is delivered to Lord John Russell, the Prime Minister. *Punch* 1848, vol.2.

72. A physical force Chartist. *Punch* 1848, vol.2

73. Ultra-Tory MP Charles de Laet Waldo Sibthorp (1783 - 1855) on discovering that he had signed the Chartist petition. On the evening of 10 April 1848, he expressed his regret to O'Connor that the outcome for the demonstrators had not been 'the damnedest hiding mortal man ever received'. *Punch* 1848, vol.2

74. A special constable dries his gunpowder. *Punch* 1848, vol.2.

75. The Chartists and the police as seen by George Cruikshank (1792 -
1878) in the *Comic Almanack*, 1848.

— FOUR-ARMED.

76. Ernest Jones (1819 - 1869). A late recruit to Chartism, Jones was educated in Germany and translated a number of French and German revolutionary poems in his various journals. He wrote poems himself, as well as a number of novels. He was imprisoned in 1848-50 and after his release struggled to keep the Chartist movement alive. At the end of his life he was building bridges towards popular Liberalism.

77. Samuel Kydd (1815 - 1892). Originally by trade a shoemaker, he wrote, under the pseudonym 'Alfred', a substantial *History of the Factory Movement*. After some years as an active Chartist leader, he qualified as a barrister and was called to the Bar in 1861, where he made a successful career. In his later years he moved towards a version of the Tory radicalism of his earlier hero, Richard Oastler.

78. John Bedford Leno (1826 - 1894). One of the post - 1848 Chartist leaders, Leno edited, with fellow-poet Gerald Massey, the *Uxbridge Spirit of Freedom*. In the 1860s he was prominently involved in the Reform League. He often sung in public, and was also not without talent as a cricketer. *The Commonwealth*, 6 October 1866.

79. W. H. Chadwick (1829 - 1908). Imprisoned at the age of nineteen for sedition and conspiracy, Chadwick maintained his Chartist convictions - and proudly wore his O'Connor medal - for the rest of his life. As this picture shows, the one-time actor and phrenologist worked as a van lecturer for the Liberals in the 1890's. The 'last of the Manchester Chartists' lived to participate in the Liberal election victory of 1906.

80. 'The Old Chartist' by F. Sandys, engraving in *Once A Week* (1862).
Chartists rarely disavowed their early commitment, and by the 1860s
reminiscent articles as well as obituaries in local Liberal newspapers
recorded the experience of many former Chartists. Not a few of the
editors of such journals had cut their political teeth as young Chartist
journalists.

A NOTE ABOUT IMAGES NOT INCLUDED IN THIS BOOK

During the course of our research for this book we unearthed a number of images which, for various reasons, we decided not to reproduce. In this note we would like to draw attention to some of them. We decided not to include, for example, photographs of Chartists taken in old age. It occurred to us that there very probably would be photographs in public libraries of Chartists who had in later life become involved in local government. This was the case with both Robert Cochran (1808-1897) and John Snowden (1821-1884). A long-serving leader of the Paisley Chartists, Cochran served on the town council for thirty-two years and was Provost between 1880 and 1885. Not surprisingly there are several photographs and lantern slides of him, alone and with colleagues, in Paisley Public Library. In Halifax Public Library there is a single photograph of John Snowden. It was probably taken in the 1870's when Snowden, who did not learn to write until he was forty-one, was three times elected to the Halifax School Board. Two other photographs worth noting are those of William Aitken (1814? - 1869) in Manchester Public Library and Samuel Cook (1786 - 1861) in Dudley Archives. The schoolmaster Aitken sits somewhat apprehensively in his best frock coat while Cook, four times imprisoned, sits proudly and defiantly, arms folded across his chest.

There are a few paintings of men associated with Chartism. One of the earliest of these is of J.R. Stephens, painted in 1839 by James Garside and now to be found in Astley Cheetham Art Gallery, Stalybridge. Portraits of Joshua Hobson (1810 - 1876), publisher of the *Northern Star* and later editor of the *Huddersfield Chronicle*, of Arthur O'Neill (1819 - 1896), one of the advocates of Christian Chartism, and of James Sweet, the Nottingham Chartist, can be found in, respectively, Huddersfield Art Gallery, Birmingham Art Gallery, and Nottingham Public Library.

We have not used all of the engravings which appeared in the periodicals of the 1840s. We reproduce here only a few of the images of the 1842 riots which were published in the *Illustrated London News*; some of the others can be found in Mick Jenkins' *The General Strike of 1842* (1980). Similarly, there is more material, particularly relating to special constables, in *Punch* for 1848. The series of portraits of delegates to the National Convention which appeared in the *Charter* for 1839 are not all reproduced. Left out of this book are depictions of John Frost (10 March 1839) and William Lovett (24 March 1839) and also of the Birmingham lamp manufacturer, Thomas Cluton Salt (3 March 1839) and the mathematician, William Villiers Sankey (14 April 1839), both of whom resigned from the Convention. The same applies to the portraits published in *Reynolds's Political Instructor* in 1850. We have not included the pictures of William Lovett (12 January 1850), Henry Hetherington (2 February 1850), Ernest Jones (23 March 1850) and Bronterre O'Brien (30 March 1850), all of whom are represented in the book by other, more interesting, images. There are two relevant pictures in *Howitt's Journal* which are not reproduced here. These are of William Lovett (vol. 1, p.253) and Perronet Thompson (vol. 2, p.65). We should also note that the *Illustrated London News* published small likenesses, including of Joseph Sturge (16 July 1842) and Thomas Duncombe (30 July 1842).

Finally, as far as events are concerned, readers may wish to know that the National Library of Wales holds a number of engravings relating to the Newport rising; and that there is a depiction of the Chartist riots in Trafalgar Square in the *Lady's Newspaper*, 11 March 1848, which is reproduced in D. Goodway, *London Chartism 1838 - 1848*, Cambridge 1982.

FURTHER READING

Those who want to read more about Chartism and its history are faced with an embarrassment of riches. Histories and accounts of the movement have been written ever since it ended, not only in Britain but in other European countries and in the U.S.A., Australia and Japan. Rather than offer a list of possibilites we refer readers to two bibliographies, two recent single volume studies and three short books which offer assessments of the main publications and include the most up-to-date material.

The bibliography by J.F.C. Harrison and Dorothy Thompson, *Bibliography of the Chartist Movement 1837 - 1976* (Sussex 1976) has been revised and up-dated in *The Chartist Movement, A New Annotated Bibliography* by Owen Ashton, Robert Fyson and Stephen Roberts (London 1995). Manuscript, archival and published material up to that date is fairly thoroughly covered in these volumes, usually with location of rare items noted.

There is no reliable narrative history of Chartism, though there are several volumes which cover the movement thematically. These include *Chartism and the Chartists by* D. J. V. Jones (London, 1975) and *The Chartists. Popular Politics in the Industrial Revolution* by Dorothy Thompson (London and New York 1984)

Three short books provide assessments and consideration of the movement and its historians.

J. R. Dinwiddy *Chartism* (Historical Association pamphlet 1987)
Edward Royle *Chartism* (London, 3rd edition 1996)
Richard Brown *Chartism* (Cambridge 1998)

THE EDITORS:

Stephen Roberts is Head of History and Law at Hagley R. C. High School, Worcestershire. He has spent many years researching and writing about Chartism.

Dorothy Thompson taught for some years in the School of History at the University of Birmingham. She has taught also in the USA, China, Japan and several European countries. She is the author of several books on Nineteenth Century British History, including *The Chartists*.